Reptile Keeper's Guides

BALL PYTHONS

R. D. Bartlett
Patricia Bartlett

BARRON'S

Acknowledgments

Our sincere thanks to the many keepers and breeders of ball pythons who have generously shared with us their expertise and allowed us to photograph their snakes or provided photos. Morph breeder Ryan Sherman (The Painted Python) provided us with wonderful photos [pages 9, 10, 11, 12, 13, 14 (top), 29], as did Chris and Sheila McQuade (Gulf Coast Reptiles) [pages 14 (bottom), 15, 26]. Bill and Marcia Brant of The Gourmet Rodent made certain we had plenty of normal morphs to photograph and shared their insights on marketing. Dave and Tracy Barker (Vida Preciousa) shared with us some alternate methods for inducing wild-caught ball pythons to feed. Rob MacInnes of Glades Herp shared with us his experiences in dealing with imports. Photos on page 16 and page 18 were provided by Travis Cossette.

All inquiries should be addressed to:
Barron's Educational Series, Inc.
250 Wireless Boulevard
Hauppauge, NY 11788
www.barronseduc.com

Library of Congress Catalog Control Number: 2010036459

ISBN-13: 978-0-7641-4589-6
ISBN-10: 0-7641-4589-4

Library of Congress Cataloging-in-Publication Data
Bartlett, Richard D., 1938–
  Ball pythons / R. D. Bartlett, Patricia Bartlett. — 2nd ed.
    p. cm.
  Includes bibliographical references and index.
  ISBN-13: 978-0-7641-4589-6
  ISBN-10: 0-7641-4589-4
  1. Ball pythons as pets. I. Bartlett, Patricia Pope, 1949– II. Title.

SF459.S5B36 2010
639.3'9678—dc22   2010036459

Printed in China
9 8 7 6 5 4 3 2 1

Contents

Preface

This book is designed to help you with the A to Z husbandry of one of the most eagerly sought and readily available of the pythons. This is the ball python, a tropical west and central African snake of relatively placid demeanor and chubby girth. There is but a single, non-subspeciated, immensely powerful, but relatively small and secretive form. If acquired when young, most ball pythons are easily kept. They are now being captive bred for the pet industry. Although many allow handling, most do not enjoy it, and excessive handling of a not-yet-fully-acclimated ball python may result in the snake refusing to feed. Not surprisingly, wild-collected adults are often less comfortable about being handled—and in fact, are usually far more difficult captives all around—than captive-bred babies.

Although we feel that the ball python is more a terrarium species than a true-pet snake, acclimated specimens tolerate some handling and remain in great demand by both new hobbyists and seasoned herpetoculturists. These are long-lived snakes (living upwards of 20 years) and their acquisition should not be taken lightly. We hope that the information we have provided will make it a little easier to understand these snakes.

Dick and Patti Bartlett
Gainesville, Florida, USA

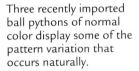

Three recently imported ball pythons of normal color display some of the pattern variation that occurs naturally.

Introduction

In the ten years since the first edition of our ball python book, this little snake has risen from comparative obscurity to a reptile prominence equaled only by the corn snake and the California kingsnake.

A decade ago the pet industry depended largely on wild-collected ball pythons of normal color to supply their moderate needs. Because many wild-collected ball pythons refused to feed or fed only sparingly in captivity, they were rightly considered by most hobbyists a snake species that was difficult to acclimate.

But due to the mystique of being a python, this alone being an immea-

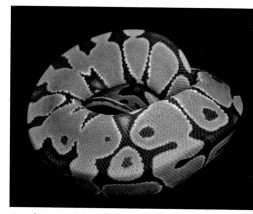

A pale orangish coloration typifies the hypomelanistic "orange ghost" color morph of ball python.

This is a pretty and alert normal-colored ball python.

Ready to emerge: the top of this hatching egg was removed to make viewing possible by attendees of a "herp-expo."

surable draw to many hobbyists, those that survived were coveted and pampered by their owners.

Breeding began, on a basis we thought was well thought out, but that seems almost laughable now. As techniques became more streamlined, a very occasional aberrantly colored and/or patterned hatchling was produced, and we all sat back and said, "Whoa! I wonder if . . . " Ball python–mania took over the breeding end of the hobby.

While normal wild-colored hatchlings of this little dark brown on warm brown snake sell for a very affordable $35 each, "high-end" aberrancies get a lot of attention. A few years ago we noticed at the big Daytona Beach Captive Breeders Expo a cup containing a newly developed pale-colored morph of ball python bearing a price tag of $30,000! Other ball python morphs on the same table ranged from $5,000 to $25,000.

As of mid 2010, with nearly 100 color and pattern morphs now available to hobbyists, and with more aberrancies being bred than ever before, prices have moderated somewhat on even the high-end ball python morphs. But whether a high-end color morph or a normal ball python, these appealing snakes deserve the best of care throughout their multi-decade life span.

What Is a Ball Python?

Ball pythons are members of the family Boidae (boas and pythons), and are contained within the subfamily Pythoninae. With only a single exception (the New World python, *Loxocemus bicolor*), pythons are Old World snakes. All are egg-layers, but aside from that, the group is a study in contrasts. Only one (the burrowing python, *Calabaria reinhardtii*), is a truly proficient burrower. Many pythons climb readily, but one (the green tree python, *Morelia viridis*), is extensively arboreal and seldom descends from the trees. Most pythons are excellent swimmers (such as the brown water python, *Liasis fuscus*). A few attain gigantic proportions (such as the Burmese python, *Python molurus bivittatus*), most are of moderate size, and a few (the Perth python, *Liasis perthensis*), are less than a yard in length when adult.

Like the related boas, pythons retain remnants of the pelvic girdle and have visible, movable pelvic spurs, one on each side of the vent. The spurs of males are usually larger than those of females. The spurs are used in breeding stimulation and to a lesser degree in territorial disputes.

The ball python is a species of moderate length (4 to 6 feet) and heavy girth. It currently is abundant in the wild. Between 30,000 and 50,000 specimens are annually provided to the American pet market trade, mostly in the form of hatchlings from wild-caught gravid females.

Imported, wild-caught specimens of the ball python can be perplexingly difficult to acclimate to captivity. Captive bred and hatched specimens are usually quite easily kept. Because imported ball pythons are inexpensive, herpetoculturists have had little financial incentive to breed the snakes

This dark ball python lacks yellow pigment and is, therefore, axanthic.

In appearance, the Angolan python, *Python anchietae*, looks much like a photo-negative image of the ball python, with the raised central portion of the scale giving a beaded feel. Short and stout, this 4- to 5-foot-long python (record, 5 feet, 11 inches) was once one of the most uncommon snakes in American collections. However, it is now represented in the collections of many zoological gardens and a dozen or so private hobbyists. An increasing number of young are available in the pet marketplace each year, but prices asked remain astronomically high—$7,500 for a pair seems to be typical. The availability is not likely to increase quickly, for the Angolan python is a slow breeder, having small numbers of relatively large eggs.

Similar to the ball python, *P. anchietae* imprints on specific rodent prey items, favoring gerbils, jirds, and certain species of rats. However, those now captive readily eat domestic rodents.

In appearance, the rare Angolan python is like a negative of the ball python. The Angolan python has been bred in captivity but remains an expensive species.

in captivity. However, the financial outlook of breeding projects with aberrantly colored morphs is far more lucrative and is currently being heavily exploited.

With a record life span of more than forty-seven years, the ball python may well be the longest-lived snake; if not, it certainly is among those that are. A more average life span would be twenty to thirty-five years. They are reproductively active for most (perhaps all) of their adult years.

Ball pythons are in nearly every pet shop in America, and until 1997 they were only somewhat less available in Europe.*

Ninety-nine percent of the ball pythons that appeared in the pet trade were imported from western Africa. For years, most specimens were wild collected and exported to overseas marketplaces almost immediately.

Realizing that exporting gravid females simply put additional money into a buyer's pockets, ball python exports began "ranching" their gravid females. This means that the gravid females were held by African collectors until they laid their eggs. The eggs were incubated and hatched, and both the hatchlings and the adults were exported. And, lo and behold, these babies were much less fussy feeders than the adults. This made the pet stores happy and their snake-buying customers happy, who then told their friends what a great pet the baby ball pythons made. As ball pythons became more popular, more were collected and the price began to drop.

Recently, some of the regulations governing ranching techniques have changed. In the 1990s, the African countries of Ghana, Togo, and Benin all were ranching ball pythons. Ghana now collects a tax on each egg collected and for each python exported. A percentage of the hatched young must be released into the wild each year. The wildlife department also charges for collecting and releasing the female pythons after they have laid their eggs, ensuring to some degree a renewable resource, at least in Ghana.

But the fact remains that tens of thousands of ball pythons are removed from the wild each year for the pet market. They are also collected and exported to Asian food markets. One must wonder how many years such vast numbers can be imported before the wild populations are irreversibly depleted.

This group of hatchling ball pythons were only a few of the many thousands of "farmed" examples imported from Africa each year.

---

*In 1997 Europe forbade the importation of ball pythons.

Ball Pythons as Pets

The ball python remains one of the least expensive and most readily available of the many python species, and it is frequently touted as the perfect pet snake. However, ball pythons are famous (or infamous) for not feeding. If you are considering the purchase of one, we urge that you insist on a feeding captive-born baby, or at least see the snake eat on two or more occasions. If these criteria are followed, a ball python can be one of the most satisfactory of the python species available in today's pet trade.

The scientific name of the ball python is *Python regius*, which translates to "royal python." This is the name that is used most frequently in European countries, but only

occasionally in America. The term *ball* comes from this python's habit of rolling into a tight ball when frightened, with its head in the center and protected by the body coils. A balled-up ball python is rather a charming sight, but they rapidly learn that this behavior doesn't discourage human touch, and may discontinue the practice.

Because of its small size (4 to 5 feet—the record is just an inch or two over 6 feet), the ball python does not, when adult, exceed the ever-burgeoning number of "6 feet and out" snake regulations being promulgated by America's communities. Yet the fact that the snake is a python, and a heavy-bodied python at that, means it still shares the mystique associated with big snakes. Additionally, because the ball python is usually placid and is reluctant to bite, it is often the snake species used to desensitize ophiophobes who wish to work on overcoming their fear of serpents or as a first snake for a neophyte hobbyist.

The ball python is primarily terrestrial, but can and does occasion-

When this hatchling ball python was photographed at the Captive Breeders' Expo in Daytona Beach, Florida, it had not yet been designated by strain.

ally climb. The majority of the ball pythons that appear in the pet industry are collected in, or at least shipped from, the African countries of Ghana and Togo. There, it inhabits scrub and semiarid land areas. It frequently follows its prey items (rodents and other small mammals) far back into their burrows. Eggs may be deposited in suitably moist, humid areas of unused mammal burrows as well as in other locations where the humidity and temperature are stable.

T negative (T−) albinism is typified by rich creamy yellow markings against a white background. The eyes are red.

Obtaining Your Ball Python

Ball pythons can be obtained from several sources. Normally colored (usually imported) specimens are available at many pet stores for much of the year. Normally colored examples are also available from specialty dealers, at captive breeder expos, or from some breeders. Specialty dealers and breeders are good sources for some of the aberrantly patterned ball pythons, but because price is high and availability is limited, it is usually necessary to go to the breeders themselves for aberrantly colored morphs.

Pet Stores

Because normally colored ball pythons are readily available for several months of the year, they have become a staple in many neighborhood pet stores. We advocate pet stores because of their convenience and the customers' ability to discuss the snake in which they are interested on a one-to-one basis with a knowledgeable store employee. Topics such as routine care are easily covered. It is important that you learn about the feeding habits of the ball python in which you are interested. Do not purchase one that has not fed. Remember, your local pet shop is often two or even three or four times removed from the initial dealing that placed the specimen in the pet trade, so its employees can be expected to know about the snake only while it has been at their store.

Transporting Your Ball Python

Whether carrying your snake home from the pet shop, to a friend's house, to a herp meeting, or elsewhere, the snake should be enclosed in a sturdy, nonabrasive cloth bag with closely sewn edges. A double-stitched bag is better than a single-stitched, and being double-bagged is better than being in a single bag. Ball pythons (in fact, most snakes) are escape artists. They seem to be able to instinctively find the weakest seam or stitch and to push (and push, and push) against it. Often what seems at first to be an escape-proof bag will be proven otherwise. This can be particularly frustrating when the snake escapes in your car. They seem to have an affinity for hiding in dashboards, and then can go where your hands will never fit.

Reptile and Amphibian Expos

Herp expos are now held in many larger cities across the United States and are becoming popular in Europe. It seems that there is at least one somewhere in the United States on any given weekend. Some are annual events; others may be biannual or quarterly. An expo is merely a gathering of dealers and breeders under one roof. They vary from the National Reptile Breeders' Expo, which is held in Florida every August and has more than 450 tables, to some that are much smaller but nearly as comprehensive. This is where breeders of the more unusual phases of ball pythons may exhibit their prized specimens.

Breeders

Breeders may vary in size from backroom hobbyists who produce only a few normally colored ball pythons every year, to commercial breeders who are striving to produce new and unusual color or pattern variants. These breeders may or may not exhibit at herp expos. Many can be found advertising in the classified or pictorial ads sections in specialty reptile and amphibian magazines (see Special Interest Groups, page 42). Breeders usually offer parasite-free, well-acclimated specimens, and accurate information. Most keep records of genetics, lineage, fecundity, health, and/or quirks of the species with which they work, and especially of the specimens in their breeding programs.

Specialty Dealers

There are many reputable specialty dealers in America and the world. Specialty dealers deal directly with breeders (across the world) and may even be direct importers. Imported specimens are usually acclimated, have been fed, and have often been subjected to a veterinary checkup. Many such dealers both buy and sell reptiles and amphibians at herp expos.

Mail Order Purchase and Shipping

Even with today's proliferation of herp expos, the larger breeders, specialty dealers, and expos themselves are still not readily available to many small-town hobbyists. If you are a little off the beaten path, and if your local pet store cannot accommodate your wants, mail order may be the answer.

T positive (T+) albinism results in a dark-eyed, two-toned, caramel-colored ball python.

How does one go about ordering a ball python from a source other than a pet store? How does one even learn that a particular python is available?

There are several ways to learn of the availability of a certain phase of ball python.

- **World Wide Web:** By instructing your search engine to seek "ball python," you should learn of several hundred breeders, many of whom have excellent photos on their Web site.
- **Classified Ads:** Dealers and hobbyists list their available livestock in the classified ads of the several reptile and amphibian, and pet, magazines.
- **Word of Mouth:** Ask friends and fellow enthusiasts for recommendations about the reptile dealers they know of. Try to check the reliability of dealers by asking about them at nature centers, museums, zoos, or among hobbyist groups. Reptile enthusiasts are a close-knit group. You'll be surprised by how many of us know each other.

After learning that your potential supplier has a satisfactory reputation, request a price list (often available automatically on the Web). Decide what, if anything, you are going to purchase, and contact your supplier/shipper to finalize details. After the first time, you will no longer find the shipping of specimens intimidating. Understanding the system will open wide new doors of acquisition.

Color Morphs

The days when there was only one color morph of ball python are

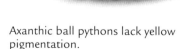

Axanthic ball pythons lack yellow pigmentation.

far behind us. Although only the "normals"—the wild colorations— are usually available in pet shops, some rather remarkable phases are now offered by specialty dealers and breeders. Some of these "new" phases do not, in themselves, do much to improve on the wild coloration, but others are startlingly different.

The normal coloration, although variable, involves a latticework of deep black/brown over a ground color of gold/tan. The lines of the dark pattern may be very thin, quite heavy, or of moderate thickness, and are usually strongly outlined with light (occasionally white) pigment of variable thickness. The head, broad and distinct from the rather slender neck, is dark on top and bears two light canthal (nose) stripes, and a posteriorly directed light subocular stripe. The head also features infrared (heat) sensitive labial pits, most prominent anteriorly.

Until the current spate of interest took hold, several of the less expensive of the fancy color phases, such as the black striped, gold striped, and jungle, were also considered normal—definable by brilliance and odd pattern, but still normal. Today, professional breeders choose the most desirable snakes from incoming shipments (selecting those with the brightest colors or most different patterns) for their breeding programs.

When you get right down to it, even the coveted and exotic-appearing piebald morphs are normal, the pattern appearing in a very small percentage of the wild ball python population.

Among other colors and patterns, the following morphs can be found on the lists of various dealers in America. Many of them occur sporadically in a clutch that produces otherwise normal hatchlings, and colors fade with age. Although the hatchlings may be truly spectacular, the adults into which they ultimately grow are of normal, or duller than normal, color.

The trouble with designer morphs of the ball pythons is the lack of standards in the names. The names we use here—provided by two com-mercial breeders—may not be the same as those used by other breeders for genetically similar animals. When you begin searching for that perfect ball python color morph, expect to find such tantalizing but somewhat non-specific names as fireball, platinum, ivory, pastel ivory, champagne, and orange crush, catchy names that pique hobbyist interest. Research, compare, research again, then decide and trea-sure the snake you have chosen.

Albinos: Although one can genetically manipulate for the trait of albinism, albinos do occur natu-rally. Albinism may take either of two forms, referred to as tyrosinase nega-tive or tyrosinase positive. Tyrosinase is a copper-containing enzyme found in plant and animal tissues that increases or decreases the produc-tion of melanin. The presence or absence of tyrosinase results in two types of albinos, tyrosinase positive or tyrosinase negative. The negative form (often written as T−) snakes are those

Piebald coloration is, perhaps, the most spectacular aberrancy yet to be seen on the ball python.

Pastel coloration can be genetically variable and has now been incorporated into the development of many new color morphs. This coloration was first noted in a wild-collected snake.

we immediately recognize as albinos, whitish creatures with red eyes (in the case of the ball python this is a buttery yellow or cream-colored snake with white lateral barring). The T positive (or T+) form allows the production of a bit of melanin, hence darker but muted colors. The tyrosinase positive ball pythons are referred to as caramels. Choose carefully; caramel ball pythons often have at least minimal spinal deformities, and your dealer might forget to tell you this.

Axanthic: A = lacking; xanthic = yellow; thus, an axanthic ball python is one that lacks the yellow pigmentation. These charcoal-on-gray ball pythons now figure increasingly in many of today's designer-colors breeding programs.

Piebald: Although you may hear of claims that albino ball pythons (T+ or T−) are the progenitors of today's designer ball pythons, the piebald form was the first. Piebalds were known in imported wild-caught snakes as far back as the early 1960s. It took another 20 years and much experimentation by the serious breeders of ball pythons (and because of the very high prices commanded by these impressive snakes, one had to be a serious breeder to justify the expense) to successfully establish this trait. We talked to one of the first producers of piebald ball pythons shortly after his first batch of potential piebalds hatched. He told us he sat by the

incubator for a day and a half, looking through the window as the eggs began to hatch. The first eggs pipped and slowly, so slowly, the first baby snake moved aside a piece of eggshell large enough to reveal the snake within. "I absolutely stopped breathing. When my eyes told my brain what they were seeing, I let out a yell that could be heard two blocks away. I did it. I had piebalds."

Piebald ball pythons may be spotted or ringed with variably sized patches of stark white. Before, after, and between the white areas the color becomes abruptly normal, but the pattern is abnormal.

Leucistic: This rare color morph is an all-white snake with blue or black eyes. The pupils are red.

Black (melanistic): The single word "black" describes this snake. The first black ball pythons known were, apparently, hatchlings from a clutch of eggs laid by a wild-caught female.

Blizzard: A blizzard is a cross between an albino black ball python and another albino black. The resulting snow-white color morph is starkly beautiful.

Striping: Dorsal striping was first noticed on imported baby ball

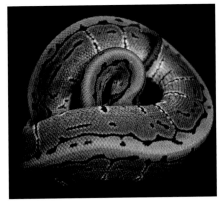

The term "pinstriping" defines ball pythons with narrow dark markings bordering a dorsal stripe and reduced lateral markings.

pythons in the 1960s, and through the ensuing years snakes having either a broad tan or chocolate brown dorsal stripe were occasionally imported (when you look at the numbers imported, roughly 50K a year for 30 years, that's a lot of snakes). Since this characteristic proved non-replicable on these imports, it was suspected that the striping was caused by sub-optimal incubation conditions, either accidentally or purposely.

Today's knowledge of genetics has resulted in replicable dorsal striping of both normal and pastel ball python variants.

One such striped form is known as the genetic striped ball python. This snake has a reduced body pattern, orange(-ish) lower sides, a precise yellowish dorsal stripe that is equally precisely dark edged, and a dark crown on the head.

The various striped pastels having a basically dark color may have a broad dark or light stripe either with or without darker edging. If edged, the edging may be narrow and precise or broad and blurred.

The stripe on the white forms is often narrow, un-edged, and of a cream or pale butter yellow color.

Mojave: The Mojave (pronounced "mo-hah-vey") mutation originated from a wild-collected example. Mojaves display a pattern of thick blackish brown dorsal and lateral markings with a pale cream-to-orange ground color and silvery gray lateral spots. Each of the light spots usually contains a dark oval or triangular spot. A mutation combining the Mojave and the spider mutations is a hazy, more golden rendition of the spider pattern. A Mojave × Mojave (a Mojave−Mojave cross) results in a super Mojave, a pure-white snake with blue eyes.

Pastel and pastel-derived forms: The pastel genes have now been incorporated into ball pythons that vary in base color from black to butter yellow. Pastels were one of the earlier genetic mutations to be replicated in captive breeding programs and was first noted

As with albinism, genetic variables may be expressed with melanistic coloration.

This snow-white blizzard strain of ball python resulted from a black × black cross, using Gulf Coast Reptiles' black ball python strain.

in wild-collected snakes. There are several independent lines producing the somewhat muted pastel coloration. It is a co-dominant coloration. The tan ground color of the normal ball python is altered to yellow (sometimes with a pale orange wash) on a pastel. Patterning is predominantly black but there is often a hint of chocolate mid-dorsally. The belly is white and the eyes are golden yellow. The breeding of a pastel with another pastel can produce ball pythons of noticeably enhanced color intensity.

Butter balls: Butter ball pythons have a pale butter yellow suffusion over the body, and when bred with a pastel may produce a hodgepodge of color morphs, including pastel, pastel butters, and normal-appearing hatchlings. The various pastels have, of course, a muted, sometimes hazy, coloration. They are similar in appearance to the lesser platinum but are genetically distinct.

Other pattern and color aberrancies: When pattern and color mutations exist together, some very desirable and beautiful (from a hobbyist viewpoint) ball pythons are produced.

One popular combination of both pattern and color aberrancy is the "pinstripe" mutation. On this mutation the black pigment is much reduced, being present only as a narrow irregular stripe on each side of the back and as variable broken lines or bars on the sides and back. This is a dominant characteristic.

Another pattern mutation is dubbed the "spider." On this variant the black markings tend to be thicker than on the pinstripe, and the paravertebral striping is less complete. Lateral markings tend to be in the form of thin bars with one or two black spots between each pair of bars. This mutation also has light green eyes (which tends to increase interest) and a "moustache." The moustache is created by a downturn of the dark rostral line, immediately before the eye. This mutation has been incorporated into many breeding programs.

For example, the spider mutation is one of the parent morphs in the very popular "bee" series, the bumble bee, the butter bee, the queen bee, and a series of others. The killer bee has a very muted body color and pattern and a smudged, almost patternless head.

Caging

A cage for an adult ball python should offer an absolutely escape-proof access, ample floor space, a secure hiding area, appropriate cage furniture, a water dish, suitable illumination, and an adequate temperature gradient. We suggest providing a cage with a floor area of at least 12 by 30 inches and 18 inches high. Depending on their design, most 30-gallon tanks will provide this.

Ball pythons may be determined in their efforts to escape. Their habit is to repeatedly seek and push, which is very effective for finding a loose cage top or a weak spot in a snake bag. Cage tops must be firmly clipped in place, and we suggest using at least four clips on each top.

While trying to escape, ball pythons may abrade their nose on a rough wire top. They seem less apt to push hard—or less able to develop leverage—against a top 18 inches above floor level than against one only a foot above floor level.

Large plastic blanket boxes, although lower than we prefer, can work quite well for ball python caging. They should have rather large air holes drilled (or melted) from the inside. Although the tops have "catches" to prevent them from being easily dislodged, these provide no challenge for a ball python determined to escape. The top may be more securely held in place by using Velcro strips on each corner. Ball pythons seem less apt to push strongly against these solid tops than against the wire top of a standard aquarium-turned-terrarium.

Several thicknesses of newspapers, although not particularly aesthetic, make an inexpensive, easily cleaned cage flooring and are absolutely nonintrusive. Layers of more highly

Racked plastic cages of various sizes are often chosen by ball python breeders.

16

This easily cleaned plastic tub provides a young ball python with a clean substrate, a hide box, and water. The ease of access for the keeper is a bonus.

absorbent paper towels are also suitable, but are likely to be pushed to the side or crumpled into a corner by the prowlings of your python. Many breeders use shredded aspen for substrate; it tends to clump around stools and water spills, and spot cleaning is relatively easy.

Cypress bark mulch and fir bark (orchid bark) are also widely used, comparatively inert substrates (unlike cedar mulch, which is not inert and should never be used). The only problem that we found with cypress mulch is that ball pythons, being rather "sloppy" eaters, tend to ingest it, or get pieces hung in their teeth when they are feeding. No intestinal impactions ever resulted, but the bits of mulch caught in the teeth can cause irritation and mouth rot. If this happens, you'll need to open the cage, pick the snake up and manually remove the mulch. Other substrates are easier in the long run.

Although ball pythons can quickly destroy many marginally sturdy objects, we almost always keep a large flat pot of snake plant or sansevieria in a corner of each cage. The plants are left potted so they can be easily moved and rotated as necessary. Artificial plants are an alternative. A live potted plant will raise the humidity in a cage and will need rather strong lighting to survive. Artificial plants, on the other hand, are just there. They need no care, other than an occasional cleaning, but neither do they contribute much except some sort of rather artificial relief to the starkness of a caging setup.

Lighting

Mention lighting to most reptile keepers, and before you know what is happening you're in the middle of a heated discussion over the benefits

Rigid plastic racks for these tub-cages are available commercially. Note the many drilled (or melted) ventilation holes in every cage.

and disadvantages of incandescent vs. fluorescent vs. actinic lighting, UV-A vs. UV-B, wavelength and full-spectrum lighting. Your simple, affordable design for ball python caging seems as if it is hurtling toward something costly.

Relax. Ball pythons in the wild spend their days in burrows and their active nights looking for food or a ball python of the opposite sex. You don't need to provide full-spectrum lights or any kind of fancy light at all. Incandescent would be good for viewing and for a little heat, but be certain to shield the bulb so a determined ball python cannot possibly come in direct contact with it and become burned.

You could opt for a compact fluorescent or a tank-top reflector equipped with a fluorescent tube light to provide light for viewing (you can provide heat via an undertank heater, but heating options are discussed in the next section).

No matter what type of lighting you choose, it should be used prudently to provide a "normal" photoperiod (day/night cycle) for your latitude. That's all it has to do. A simple timer, changed weekly to reflect current sunrise and sunset times as listed in your local paper, will help provide normal photoperiod in rooms without outside windows. A general rule is to provide 12 hours of light, followed by 12 hours of darkness.

Heating

Since ball pythons hail from equatorial areas, it is necessary for some sort of safe heat source to be incorporated into their cages.

Ceramic heaters are now available that merely screw into an everyday incandescent light socket. Some of these emit a considerable amount of heat and last for extended periods. Care must be used to make sure your snake cannot come in direct contact with the heating element and burn itself. Heat lamps are also frequently used. These not only heat the air, but when close enough to a solid object (rock, shelf, cage floor) will heat it as well. Again, care must be used to make sure the python cannot come in contact with, or close enough to, the bulb to burn itself. Your goal is daytime temperatures of 81–85°F and nighttime temperatures of 79–81°F.

An ever expanding array of under-tank/undercage heaters, heating cables, heating pads, "hot rocks" and other heat-emitting paraphernalia is becoming available. Some have thermostats already built in, and the rest can be attached to rheostats. These heating gadgets all have the advantage of providing a warmed substrate (cage bottom or shelf) of a defined area upon which the snake can lie and directly thermoregulate. This may be a more satisfactory method than just generally heating the entire cage, for it will allow the snake to find the most suitable temperature within the thermal gradient.

Although important to all specimens, suitable temperature regulation is especially important to ovulating, gestating, or incubating female ball pythons.

Hide Boxes

Ball pythons are one of the shyer and more retiring of the medium-sized boids. Hide boxes are mandatory for the long-term management of these pythons. A feeling of security may well determine whether a ball python—even a fairly well acclimated ball python—eats or not.

Many types and designs of commercial hide boxes are readily available. Most of these are made from easily washable and sterilizable plastics. Some even have a water dish built into their tops, but since ball pythons are so adept at overturning objects, we do not use these.

If they are of suitable diameter, tubes or sections of cork bark are also ideal. These, too, are fairly easy to clean and may be soaked in a weak bleach solution to sterilize them. Ball pythons seem to like them best if one of the ends is closed. This is informally and easily accomplished by wedging a slightly oversized piece of cork into the end.

Some hobbyists, striving for inexpensive convenience, merely use

Remember that even captive hatched ball pythons are shy snakes and must be provided with a hide box. This enclosure needs a hide box.

Adult ball pythons will require large tubs, cages, or terraria. Cage furniture such as driftwood or plastic stands may be used if provided. Affix the furniture so that it will not harm the snake if it is dislodged.

Hide boxes, and their placement in the cage, should be tailored to your specimen(s).

Ball pythons seem more secure if they have their body surfaces in contact with the inside of their hiding area. Thus, a large box for a small snake, while allowing the animal to get out of sight, will not give the same feeling of security as a smaller box will.

Water

We are of the opinion that ball pythons need only an occasional soak, and this is most beneficial when your snake is preparing for ecdysis. The size and volume of the water dish/receptacle used in any cage will need to be determined by the size and type of snake for which it is intended. Water dishes should be untippable. The heavy crockery dishes sold in feed and pet stores for dogs and other animals are ideal in most cases. They are low and easily cleaned, sterilized, and rinsed, often have a lip (which acts as a partial squeegee, ridding your snake of some excess water droplets as it crawls over or through), and are inexpensive, sturdy, and readily available in a great many sizes.

suitably sized cardboard boxes with an entrance hole cut in one side for hide boxes. These are thrown away and replaced when soiled.

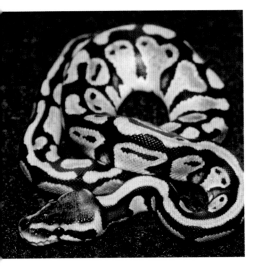

In today's world of designer ball pythons, this well-marked imported example would undoubtedly be incorporated into a sophisticated breeding program.

Feeding

Throughout their lives, ball pythons feed predominantly on warm-blooded prey. Although this may sound like a straightforward and easily accommodated diet (and often it is), some ball pythons—especially adults collected from the wild—can be exasperatingly difficult to induce to feed.

We feel that the reasons for this are severalfold and involve very different causes, all of which must eventually be overcome if the snake is to thrive in captivity.

To begin, let's define the causes. Important among them is the weeks of progressively more debilitating conditions an adult ball python has sustained following collection. During the several weeks following its collection until it appears for sale in your pet store, the ball python has been kept in unnatural quarters (usually with other ball pythons, sometimes with other snake species), been bagged and unbagged (up to several times), experienced varying (sometimes adverse) temperatures, been deprived of suitable food and clean water and normal photoperiod, and, because of these stresses, experienced a proliferation of internal parasites.

Secondly, ball pythons in the wild often undergo one or more periods of inactivity and fasting annually. This is normal, and the duration of each fast is variable.

Thirdly, wild ball pythons "prey imprint." That is, they prefer (at times, insist on!) the particular kind of prey animal on which they fed in the wild. This may be a gerbil or other rodent species not available in the pet trade.

Although any one of the above problems could be difficult for a hobbyist to overcome, surmounting two or three of them can call to the forefront every shred of herpetocultural expertise that you have.

Hatchling ball pythons ranched in Africa typically undergo fewer stresses before being shipped, are physiologically ready to accept their

Reluctant feeders may accept prey placed in the opening of a hide box after darkness has fallen.

Here are some suggestions to entice your ball python to eat:

- Be sure your ball python is well hydrated. If dehydration is advanced, Gatorade or Pedialite, administered orally daily by entubation (15 ml per kg of body weight) may be necessary to correct the problem (see Health, pages 33–41).

- Be certain that endoparasites are not a problem (consult a veterinarian. See also Health, pages 33–41).

- Provide your python with a hide box in which it can feel secure. A secure snake will feed more readily than a nervous one.

- Allow your ball python a minimum of two weeks to acclimate.

- Ascertain that temperature and humidity are as close to "ideal" as you can get them.

- Profferring a prekilled mouse with its brain exposed may induce a reluctant snake to feed.

- Some snakes may feed more readily on live than on dead prey, and some may prefer just the opposite. Experiment. Do not leave live prey unattended.

- Some snakes feed more readily on newly born prey than on older animals.

- Try feeding your ball python live baby or prekilled prey in a darkened (but adequately ventilated), restricted space such as a paper bag or cardboard shoe box. Alternate prey types.

- In conversation, python breeder David Barker has suggested a method of enticement with which we are not familiar. Barker suggests putting a baby rat or gerbil (with its bedding) in a plastic bucket with an access hole cut a little above ground level. This apparently simulates near-natural conditions to a hungry and hunting ball python and may induce the snake to eat.

- If in reasonable condition, ball pythons are quite capable of going for several weeks, or even several months, without feeding. However, they must drink more frequently, and endoparasites can sap their resources. Rather than responding favorably to tease-feeding as many other pythons and boas do, ball pythons are likely to coil and hide their head. Do not force-feed until absolutely necessary.

- If it does become necessary to force-feed your snake, use a small syringe and a soft rubber tube or a "pinky pump." Vitamin-enhanced semiliquid, all-meat baby food is a good first choice. Use extreme care, for at best, force-feeding is a traumatic experience for your snake.

Whether the prey is offered alive (not suggested) or freshly killed (preferred), a ball python will usually constrict it before beginning the swallowing process.

Beginning the swallowing process ...

first meal, and have not yet become prey-imprinted, criteria that make them better candidates than the adults for successful captive husbandry.

Better by far than even these African-ranched babies are baby ball pythons that have been domestically bred. Although these may be somewhat more expensive, they (and usually generations before them) have undergone far fewer stresses and are already accustomed to eating laboratory mice and rats.

Is there an answer to the feeding problems often posed by ball pythons imported from Africa?

The very best course of action is not to purchase the snake until you have seen it eat at least twice. (We suggest twice, with at least a week in between, for sometimes newly imported ball pythons will eat once, and not again.) We consider this of the utmost importance when you are considering the purchase of an imported adult, and strongly urge that you see an imported baby eat at least once. Accurate feeding records kept by a store, dealer, or breeder that you trust

would be as good as actually viewing the feeding. Do keep in mind, though, that most baby ball pythons will not feed until after they have had their postnatal shed. This is normal.

If you somehow have acquired a ball python that refuses to feed, first ascertain that the cage temperature is suitable, that your snake has a secure hide box, that you are not handling the snake unnecessarily (handling can throw a nervous ball python off feed), that the python is well hydrated, and that endoparasites are not at significant levels. If these criteria are met, begin experimenting with all manner and color of available food species. Try gerbils, mice, small rats, and hamsters. Try them all both alive and prekilled, although prekilled prey needs to be your eventual goal. When you attempt the live prey, introduce it in the early evening (don't leave the snake and prey untended, though). When you try prey items dead, first warm them (not in a microwave oven!) to normal body temperature. This is easily done in warm water (blot dry before placing in the cage) or under the heat of a reflector and bulb. Then place the food item in the door of your snake's hide box. Sometimes exposing the brain of a prekilled animal will induce your snake to eat. Sometimes washing the animal (to rid it of its natural odor) then drying it before offering it will work. As you eliminate one after the other of these methods and your ball python still refuses to accept food, you will probably be ready to agree that ball pythons are not the fail-safe pet species that they are often cracked up to be! You'll agree entirely if it finally becomes necessary to force-feed your specimen to save it from its self-imposed fast.

Commercial breeders of mice and rats exist in many areas. From these breeders, feeder animals may be purchased either live or frozen (we prefer and recommend the latter). Many such suppliers advertise in the classified sections of reptile magazines. Feeder rodents may also be purchased from many pet stores and reptile dealers, or you may raise them.

Live Versus Dead Mice

Contrary to belief, most snakes neither need, nor even seem to prefer, live food over dead. We feed once-frozen, fully thawed and warmed mice to 100 percent of our snakes. Captive snakes can be shy creatures that feel at a disadvantage when confronted with live prey in a confined space. In the wild, the snake is the aggressor, sitting concealed and quietly in wait next to a rodent trail, or actively trailing its prey. In a cage, a live rodent (or a baby chick) can become the aggressor. In the confines of a cage, small rats have been known to injure—even to kill—adult ball pythons. Eye and tongue injuries and ultimate loss, lip and mouth injuries resulting in mouth rot, and even body injuries occur all too often. Once intimidated by a rapid approach, or a bite from a prey rodent, most ball pythons will never bite their intended prey. If for some reason you feel you must feed live rodents to your snakes, never leave the cage unmonitored while the live rodent is present.

We usually allow the pythons to tell us they are hungry before we attempt to feed them. When hungry, ball pythons will either prowl continually about their cage or sit with head extended from the hide box seeming to watch near-cage movements more alertly than when sated. These snakes are more apt to feed in the early evening than at any other time of day.

It is *very* important that the food animals be thoroughly thawed before being eaten by the snake. We do not thaw rodents in a microwave. Not only is the thawing uneven (creating pockets of intense heat while leaving other spots frozen), but microwaving further weakens an already weakened body wall, often making the rodent entirely unusable. We usually present the rodents to the ball pythons nose first, in long hemostats, laying them in the door of the hide box after thawing them in hot water. Most are readily accepted.

Could gravity actually help? This baby seems to believe so.

Breeding

Although readying your ball pythons for breeding involves more than simply putting the two sexes together, it is not a difficult task. Certainly you'll need both sexes, but ball pythons are fairly easily sexed. Observing their appearance is one way to sex them. The males have a bulge (called the *hemipenial bulge* because it houses the sexual organs or the hemipenes) at the base of their tails, in the area of the vent, and their tails taper rapidly after the vent. Females have no hemipenial bulge, and their tails are longer and taper less rapidly.

Probing is the second way. Ball pythons are a short-tailed python. Although males do have larger pelvic spurs and a thicker tail than the females, the sexes are still confusingly

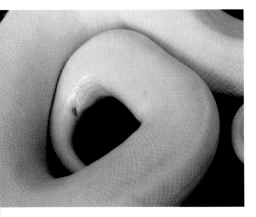

similar externally. Probing is the most reliable way of accurately sexing your ball pythons. In this technique, a lubricated probe of suitable diameter is inserted first into the cloaca of the snake. The tip of the probe is then urged gently rearward along the tail. If the ball python is a male, the probe will enter the hemipenial sheath to a distance of about 10 subcaudal scales (use extreme care when performing this). If the snake is a female it will only probe about 3 subcaudal scales deep. Have a knowledgeable herpetoculturist demonstrate the technique and, until you feel confident, actually probe your snakes.

Greatest breeding success occurs if you keep the sexes separated except during their winter breeding season and if during the time they are together you follow the rhythm of the seasons in cycling the snakes.

If you normally house your pair together, we suggest that you separate them for at least two weeks prior to the breeding season. When the breeding season begins, place the snakes in the same cage. Reproductive interest is often greater than normal during

The yellowish anal spurs may be easily seen against the snow white of this blizzard ball python.

periods of atmospheric low pressure, such as during the passage of fronts, hurricanes, and other storms. Misting your snakes may stimulate them. The temporary placing of a second sexually mature male specimen with the pair is also a stimulant. Territorial defense and combat will usually ensue, often changing to a breeding response along the way.

The same pair may breed several times during each cycle. Breeding may occur from the day the pair is introduced through mid-March. Ovulation causes a midbody swelling, and most females will again cease eating from this point until egg deposition. About three weeks prior to egg deposition, the female ball python will shed her skin.

Ball pythons lay small clutches of large eggs. A clutch from an average-sized, healthy female numbers from three to eight (occasionally fewer, rarely two or three more). At a temperature of 87–90°F (with a 90–95 percent relative humidity), incubation will last for about two months.

The Deposition Site

Secure and well-acclimated ball pythons breed most readily. A hide box and other visual barriers (vertical panels, horizontal shelves, perches, plants) will enhance your snake's feeling of security.

Gestating ball pythons need warm, secure areas in which to bask, and ultimately, to deposit their eggs.

An opaque plastic tub partially filled with barely moistened peat or sphagnum will often be accepted for the deposition of eggs (although almost as often, your female ball python will be found in the morning

This tangle of ball python color morphs were on display at the Captive Breeder's Expo in Daytona Beach, Florida.

coiled around a clutch that she has deposited on the dry floor of the cage). The deposition chamber becomes even more desirable to the snake if it is covered, either by inverting and securing a second tub above the first or by placing the tub in a darkened cardboard box. In both cases, be sure to cut an appropriately sized access hole.

The deposition tub can be set on top of a heating cable or pad (set on low) to increase warmth. Remember that heat from beneath will quickly dry the sphagnum (or other medium) and that remoistening this on a regular basis will be necessary.

Artificial Incubation

Female ball pythons will usually attempt to incubate their clutch, but do not seem to have the ability to raise their body temperature above that of the ambient by shivering. Instead, they will periodically leave the clutch, bask in a warmed area, then return and warm the clutch by making full contact with their body coils. If an incubating captive female python finds it necessary to leave her clutch frequently to elevate her body temperature, the temperature at the incubation site may be just a little too low. The parameters you provide will, of course, be directly responsible for the success or failure of any viable eggs laid by your snakes.

Although maternal incubation is interesting, we have found it difficult to provide the criteria needed throughout the two-month incubation period. We strongly urge artificial incubation of the clutch. You can buy an effective incubator for reptile eggs for about $150 and up. (Yes, there are less expensive models, but temperature/humidity control is quite iffy. You get what you pay for.)

The eggs are placed in a sweater box or large refrigerator container, atop an inch or so of dampened incubation medium. The medium can be either vermiculite or sphagnum (we prefer the latter). Dampen the medium ahead of time by adding warm water to the medium and stirring until it sticks together. Then take handfuls of the medium and squeeze out the excess water, and then squeeze

The temperatures in this reliable homemade incubator are regulated by an external Spyder Robotics thermostat.

Seeing this clutch of hatching lemonblasts and pinstriped pastels would gladden the heart of any breeder of ball pythons.

again. The medium is to be damp, not wet.

Nestle the eggs in the medium. If the eggs stick together, move them as a unit. Keep the same side of the eggs up as you move them. Place the lid on the container, and put the container in the incubator. When you check the eggs, every day or every other day, open the top and allow air exchange.

How do you know if the eggs are fertile or viable? Soon after being laid, those eggs that are not fertile will turn yellow, harden, and begin to collapse. Should embryo death occur during incubation, discoloration often soon follows. Fertile eggs will remain white and turgid to the touch until about two weeks prior to hatching, when they will begin dimpling. Infertile eggs, if not adherent to others, should be removed and discarded.

At the end of the incubation period—which may vary in duration from fifty-five to sixty-two days—the baby ball pythons will pip.

The babies may remain in the pipped egg for as long as a day and a half. Once they have hatched, they should be moved to another terrarium and offered a warmed hiding spot and water. They should shed within a few days, and most will feed soon thereafter.

With passing time, more captive breeding programs will provide us with an increasing percentage of domestically raised specimens. As this happens, the pet industry's not inconsiderable pressures on wild populations will lessen.

Additionally, as more are produced, the price of aberrant specimens will diminish somewhat. But since ball pythons have very small clutches, it will be many years before some of the most unusual variants drop sufficiently in price to become pet shop items.

Seasonal Preparation

There are many techniques designed to induce breeding—this is just one of them.

Autumn-winter preparation: Start with healthy snakes with a good weight.

Select a month you'd like to use as a start date for cooling—you'll work forward from this for your other dates. Most breeders use October 1. The sexes should be in separate caging. Reduce nighttime temps by turning off the heat tape and lights with the setting sun, and turn them on again as the sun rises. Daytime cage temperatures should be in the low 70s, nighttime temps about five degrees less.

A month later (Nov. 1, if you're using this schedule), place the male with the female. They may show an immediate breeding response, or they may wait. Leave the pair together for three months, disturbing them only weekly as you

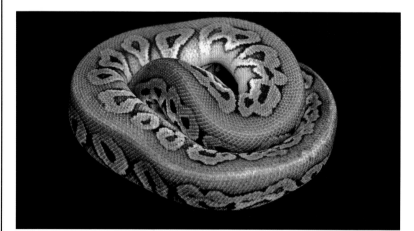

The pewter color morph has a flat, silvery sheen—and typically, the ball python conceals its head.

No matter the color, a hatchling ball python is less than a handful ...

separate them and offer food. (If you have several pairs, you can shift the males from cage to cage as part of the food offering routine.)

The snakes may or may not show any interest in food, but it's important to offer it. Males who are shifted from cage to cage and from female to female tend to become quite thin

... and a coiled adult can nestle in two hands.

The replicable color morph having a dark-edged brown dorsal stripe is referred to as a "genetic-striped" ball python.

as the result of their labors, and may not feed. If your male(s) is/are serving several females, return any that get too thin from the breeding program back to his own cage. Put him back into a regular feeding regime, undistracted by females. It may take a few weeks for him to get females out of his system and to respond to food.

By the end of January, or four months into your breeding program, those females who display a mid-body bulge are ovulating, literally making eggs. Watch your female(s) when you note the body bulge. In a few weeks those who are gravid should shed. This is called a pre-deposition shed, and it's a clear indication that in 30 days you'll have eggs—so get that incubator ready!

Health

Once acclimated, ball pythons are a hardy and easily kept species. Longevity records note a captive life of twenty to forty-seven years!

However, until fully acclimated, these snakes can be exasperatingly difficult, some exhausting the patience and creativity of their desperate owners. This is especially true if the owner is new to reptile keeping and has been led to believe that the ball python is a fail-safe species.

There are a few things that you can do to help assure the health of your ball python and your peace of mind.

1. Begin with a hatchling ball python.
2. Begin with a captive bred and hatched ball python whenever possible.
3. See the ball python you hope to purchase eat the kind of food you intend to feed it not once, but *twice*.
4. Begin with a ball python that has good muscle tone and body weight.

Choosing a Healthy Specimen

It is very important that when you select a ball python, you select a healthy, *feeding* specimen with good muscle tone and body weight, and no evidence of dehydration. These criteria may be difficult for inexperienced hobbyists to ascertain, for ball pythons are secretive, sedentary snakes that remain for long periods beneath cover. This natural quietness may make them seem less than alert when nothing could be further from the truth. This is natural behavior for a wait-and-ambush predator.

Look at the overall size and body weight of the snake. The ball python is naturally a proportionately heavy-bodied snake, and the specimen at which you are looking should show neither folds of skin nor ribs. A skin fold or "accordion" ribs indicate an unnatural thinness that may be

The scales of a ball python do not bear keels (ridges).

It is from its propensity for defensive coiling—into a ball—that gives the ball python its common name.

associated with improper diet, dehydration, or other problems.

Adult ball pythons collected from the wild are notorious for their erratic feeding behavior. This is addressed more fully in the chapter on feeding (pages 21–25), but be cautioned that this is one snake that you should see feed before purchase. Because they may eat once, then not again, we suggest that you see a ball python feed at least twice, at weekly intervals, before finalizing purchase.

When choosing a ball python, select one that displays an alert demeanor when it is disturbed. With most specimens of this snake, being alert will usually equate to being quick to roll into a ball when touched. Ball pythons are normally hardy snakes that will, if healthy at the outset, then given reasonable care, usually remain so for many years.

Shedding

A healthy, fast-growing baby ball python will shed two or three times more frequently than a slowly growing adult. Ill specimens may have difficulty shedding at all, or if shedding does occur, it is often incomplete. However, no matter its age, a ball python suffering from blister disease or other skin trauma will usually enter a rapid shed cycle in an attempt to rid itself of the problem. If the cause of the blistering (usually bacteria from overly damp or unclean quarters) is corrected, all evidence of the disease will often disappear after two or three sheds.

The shedding process (also called molting, or, more properly, ecdysis) results from thyroid activity. A week or so prior to shedding, the colors of your snake will appear to fade. As the old keratinous layer loosens from the new one forming beneath it, your ball python will take on a dull grayish or silvery sheen. Even its eyes will temporarily dull and become bluish. Besides better accommodating the growing snake, the new skin will be an improved moisture barrier over the old. The snake removes the old skin by pressing against cage furniture. When shedding has been completed, your ball python will be as brightly hued and patterned as it was to begin with.

Although snakes in the wild seldom have problems shedding, some captives may. Shedding problems may often be associated with newly imported specimens, specimens that are dehydrated or in otherwise suboptimal condition, or when the relative humidity in the ball python's cage is too low. Examine the shed skin to make sure that the eye caps (brilles) have been shed. Even when shedding is otherwise successful, the old skin may adhere to the tail tip or the eyes. If not manually (and very carefully) removed by the keeper, the dried skin can restrict circulation, resulting in the loss of the tail tip or, if on the eyes, impaired vision and eventual blindness. A drop of artificial tears or mineral oil will often loosen the brilles so they may be manually lifted free. If patches of skin adhere, a gentle misting with tepid water may help your snake rid itself of the pieces.

It is mandatory that all exfoliating skin be removed. If it does not come off easily, placing your python in a damp cloth bag, or in an aquarium with dampened crumpled cloth towels amongst and between which the snake may crawl, and leaving it overnight (make sure temperatures are between 82°F and 88°F) may loosen the skin and allow your snake to shed. Occasionally, you may have to manually help your snake rid itself of a particularly resistant shed, first loosening the adhering skin with artificial tears or mineral oil. Elevating relative humidity, occasionally misting a snake that is preparing to shed, and just general good health will often keep any problems from recurring.

Quarantine

To prevent the spread of diseases and parasites, quarantine procedures

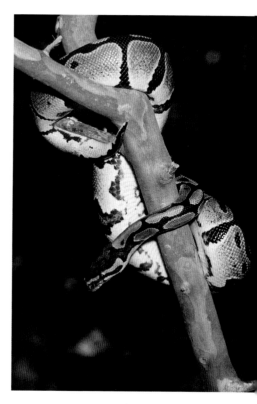

Although they seldom climb, ball pythons are quite capable of doing so.

Acclimating Your Ball Python

1. Acquire only a well-hydrated ball python.

2. If it is an import, acquire only if the ball python has fed twice with at least a week between feedings.

3. If it is domestically bred, ascertain from the breeder that the ball python has fed.

4. If it is imported, have a veterinarian assess and treat endoparasitic loads.

5. If it is imported, inspect for and remove any ectoparasites.

6. Handle only when absolutely necessary.

7. Provide secure caging.

8. Provide ideal cage temperatures.

9. Provide a secure hide box of proper size.

10. Place caging in a low-disturbance area.

11. After about two weeks, attempt to feed your snake (see chapter on feeding, pages 21–25, for suggestions).

should be of interest to anyone having more than one snake. A quarantine of one month seems best, but a week is better than no quarantine at all. During quarantine, frequent behavioral observations and other tests should be run to determine the readiness of placing the new specimen with those already being maintained. During this time, fecal exams should be carried out to determine whether or not endoparasites are present.

For this, the expertise of a qualified reptile veterinarian should be sought. The quarantine area should be completely separate from the area in which other reptiles are kept, preferably in another room.

The quarantine tank should be thoroughly cleaned prior to the introduction of the new snake(s), and it should be regularly cleaned throughout the quarantine period. As with any other terrarium, the quarantine tank

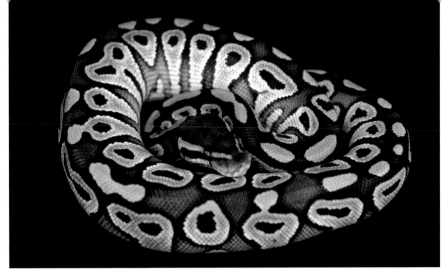

The Mojave pattern and color is a fairly new form of the ball python.

should be geared to the needs of the specimen it is to house. Temperature, humidity, size, lighting, and all other factors must be considered.

Only after you (and your veterinarian) are completely satisfied that your new specimen(s) are healthy and habituated should they be brought near other specimens.

Dehydration

Imported ball pythons are often moderately to seriously dehydrated. Dehydration is demonstrated by longitudinal and vertical folds of skin, an apparent lack of supple appearance when coiled, and by a pervasive "dried" look that will be apparent once you become familiar with snakes. If dehydration is advanced, normal drinking may not restore the balance. It is suggested that dehydration be remedied by entubating the snake daily and syringing 15 ml of plain Gatorade or Pedialite per kg of body weight into the snake's stomach until improvement is noted.

To entubate, restrain the ball python's head, and gently force the jaws open using a thin, blunt object (the rounded tip of a spoon, cupped side up); hold the mouth open by inserting a small syringe or ballpoint pen crossways; gently pass the feeding tube into the snake's esophagus for a distance of 10–12 inches. Be very certain that the tube enters the snake's throat, not the glottis (breathing opening).

Both when opening the snake's mouth and when removing the syringe or pen from its mouth, use extreme care not to break or loosen teeth or bruise gums.

Ectoparasites: Ticks and Mites

Mites and ticks are a fact of life with snakes, especially if you are purchasing or exchanging specimens.

Ticks are more easily dealt with than mites, merely because they are bigger, present in only small concen-

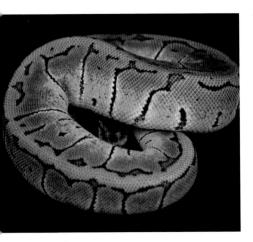

The lemonblast morph takes its name from the strong yellows in the ground color.

trations, and readily seen and removed on an individual basis. You can spot-spray a tick with a commercial reptile ivermectin spray and wait for it to die, or you can use a pair of tick removal tweezers (used for dogs and available online and in pet stores, feed stores, and some hardware stores). The tick tweezers look like cheap plastic, but they work by grasping the tick by its head, not by its body. The tweezers are then rotated—no real pulling or squeezing of the tick's body is involved—and the tick is essentially unscrewed from your snake's flesh. Crush the tick and dispose of the remains.

Mites are more difficult to combat since they're smaller and often present in large numbers. You must not only treat the snake, but its caging as well. Mite eggs hatch every nine days, so your treatment will have to be repeated in nine days to kill the new emergents.

Use a commercial reptile iver-mectin mite spray, being very careful not to get the spray in your snake's eyes or mouth, and spray the stripped caging as well. Put in new substrate,

a scrubbed hide box, a well-washed water dish, and mite-sprayed rocks, branches, and other cage furniture. Do not use any sort of multi-layer substrate during the mite treatment process. This means no mulch, no wood shavings, no leaves. You need a substrate like newspaper or paper towels, something that provides no hiding area for mites.

Repeat the spray and cage clean-ing in nine days. If this doesn't take care of your mite problem, your best bet is to take your snake to your rep-tile veterinarian for injectable ivermec-tin—again at nine-day intervals.

Stress

Whereas many snakes show stress by coiling and striking, ball pythons indicate their discomfort by balling, usually tightly, and hiding their head in the center of their coils. The balling reflex can be triggered by what might seem to be inconsequential events—a bright light, a movement above them, being handled, or being sniffed by a family pet. If a ball python is balled, it is stressed, and stress is debilitating. Wild-collected ball pythons are often more easily stressed than those that are captive bred, but all need secure, stress-free quarters.

Burns, Bites, and Abscesses

Prevention of these three prob-lems is not difficult and requires just a little forethought on the part of the keeper. Covering incandescent lightbulbs and fixtures and ascertaining that the surface of your hot rocks or blocks do not go above 95°F will eliminate the potential for burning. If your ball python is accidentally burned, cool the burned area and apply a clean dressing until you take the snake to your veterinarian.

Bites are most often from feed rodents. Despite being a top-of-the-line predator, snakes frequently get bitten, sometimes seriously so, by their prey. This happens in the wild, but apparently less often there than under captive conditions. Rats being constricted have been known to bite right through a snake's eye or to injure the glottis or nostrils. A rat or mouse left unattended in a ball python's cage might well chew holes right through the snake's body, injuring the reptile so severely that it is either permanently disfigured or must be euthanized. These examples of owner carelessness are almost everyday occurrences.

Prekill your rodents! Do not hope that your snake will make the kill cleanly and quickly. Someday it won't, and you'll be on your way to see a veterinarian, hoping that he or she will be able to correct a problem that should never have occurred to begin with. It is not macho to insist that a captive snake kill its own prey; it is dumb!

An improperly sterilized and healed burn or bite may result in the formation of an abscess. Some abscesses will eventually heal and slough off or be rubbed off; a very few may require surgical removal. Consult your reptile veterinarian.

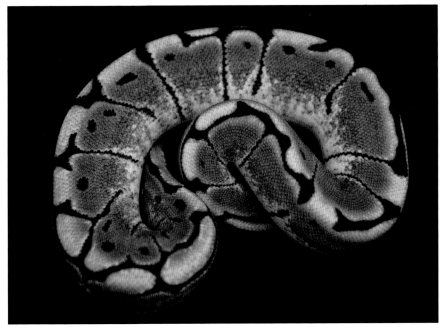

The weblike pattern is called the spider morph.

Respiratory Distress

Prolonged cold temperatures, particularly in damp situations, can cause a cold or pneumonia. Unless treated, these can be fatal. Treatments that effectively combat some respiratory problems are not necessarily equally effective against all. Likewise, a medication that works effectively on one species of snake might not work well on another. Some aminoglycoside drugs that are ideally suited for curing a given respiratory problem may be so nephrotoxic that they kill the snake if the animal is dehydrated in the least. Some respiratory problems are resistant to the old cadre of treatments . . . ampicillin, amoxicillin, tetracycline, or penicillin. Given all of these variables and the probable seriousness of the problem if the condition worsens, we feel it is mandatory that you seek the advice of a qualified reptile veterinarian at the first sign of respiratory distress. Do not wait until bubbling, wheezing, and rasping begin. To help with the cure, elevate the cage temperature to 88–95°F, and reduce relative humidity. Since some respiratory problems are communicable, quarantine the sick snake in a separate cage, preferably in a separate room.

Infectious Stomatitis (Mouth Rot)

An insidious and common disease, mouth rot must be caught and corrected at early stages to prevent permanent disfigurement. Stress, mouth injuries, and unsanitary caging conditions either alone or in combination can cause this disease. It is characterized by areas of white, cheesy-looking material along the ball python's gums. This material may be massive enough to force the lips apart. Once the material is detected, the mouth should be cleaned of any forming caseous material. Use cotton swabs to gently wipe off the exudate. Following this, wash the affected and infected areas with hydrogen peroxide. Sulfa drugs seem to be the drug of choice for treating mouth rot, but consult your reptile veterinarian for her or his recommendation. Complete eradication of mouth rot may take up to two weeks of daily treatment.

Blister Disease

Although this is usually a bacterial malady associated with dirty water and unclean quarters, blister disease sometimes crops up when the humidity in a cage is overly high or when the substrate becomes wet. First and foremost, correct the cause. Lower the humidity, sterilize the cage, and provide new, dryer substrate. If the blister disease is minimal, your ball python will probably enter a "rapid shed cycle" and divest itself of the problems within a shed or two. If the disease is advanced and has caused underlying tissue to become necrotic, it will be necessary to rupture each blister and clean the area daily (for seven to fourteen days) with diluted Betadyne and/or hydrogen peroxide. Again, your snake will enter a rapid shed cycle, and after two sheds its skin should appear normal. This can be a fatal disease if not caught and treated promptly.

The heavy dark markings provide strong contrast against the pale ground color of the desert morph.

Mention of Medical Treatments for Endoparasitism

Many reptiles, even those that are captive bred and hatched, may harbor internal parasites. Because of the complexities of identifying endoparasites and because it is necessary to accurately weigh specimens to be treated and to measure purge dosages, the eradication of internal parasites is best left to a qualified reptile veterinarian.

Handling Your Ball Python

Although many boas and pythons will allow gentle handling, ball pythons often find handling stressful and show resistance to such familiarity by adopting their characteristic balled position. We consider most ball pythons display animals only.

Many ball pythons will remain quietly in their hide box and may be moved when necessary, hide box and all.

When it is necessary to handle your ball python, do so gently, using both hands if the snake is large. Do not tap on the terrarium glass or cage front. Do not force your ball python out of its characteristic balled position. Most ball pythons are reluctant to bite, but if your snake does bite you, do not yank your hand roughly from its mouth. If you do, you will not only worsen your own wounds, but you are apt to break the teeth and injure the gums of your python. Such injury may result in "mouth rot" (infectious stomatitis), which can be difficult to cure and fatal if not treated. A second admonition: Do not drop your snake. A drop can result in damage to internal organs or broken bones.

Learn the dos and don'ts of snake handling by watching and asking experienced keepers. Your ball python will appreciate your efforts.

Special Interest Groups

Herpetological Societies

Reptile and amphibian interest groups have their own clubs, monthly magazines, and professional societies.

Herpetological societies (or clubs) exist in major cities in North America, Europe, and other areas of the world. Most have monthly meetings, some publish newsletters, and many organize or sponsor field trips, picnics, or various other interactive functions. Among the members are enthusiasts of varying expertise. Information about these clubs can often be learned by querying pet shop employees, high school science teachers, university biology professors, or curators or employees at herpetology departments at museums and zoos. All such clubs welcome inquiries and new members.

Two of the professional herpetological societies are

Society for the Study of Amphibians and Reptiles (SSAR)
www.ssarherps.org

Herpetologists' League
www.herpetologistsleague.org

The SSAR publishes two quarterly journals: *Herpetological Review* contains husbandry, range extensions, news on ongoing field studies, and so on, whereas the *Journal of Herpetology* contains articles oriented more toward academic herpetology.

A hobbyist magazine that publishes articles on all aspects of herpetology and herpetoculture is

Reptiles
P.O. Box 6050
Mission Viejo, CA 92690

Baby farmed and imported ball pythons of normal coloration are now very inexpensive in the pet trade.

Glossary

Aestivation: A period of warm weather inactivity; often triggered by excessive heat or drought.

Albino: Lacking black pigment.

Ambient temperature: The temperature of the surrounding environment.

Anal plate: Large scute (or scutes) covering the snake's anus.

Anterior: Toward the front.

Anus: The external opening of the cloaca; the vent.

Brille: The transparent "spectacle" covering the eyes of a snake.

Brumation: The reptilian and amphibian equivalent of mammalian hibernation.

Caudal: Pertaining to the tail.

cb/cb: Captive bred, captive born.

cb/ch: Captive bred, captive hatched.

Chorioallantois: The gas-permeable membranous layer inside the shell of a reptile egg.

Cloaca: The common chamber into which digestive, urinary, and reproductive systems empty and which itself opens exteriorly through the vent or anus.

Constricting: To wrap tightly in coils and squeeze.

Crepuscular: Active at dusk and/or dawn.

Deposition: As used here, the laying of eggs or birthing of young.

Deposition site: The spot chosen by the female to lay her eggs or have young.

Dimorphic: A difference in form, build, or coloration involving the same species; often sex-linked.

Diurnal: Active in the daytime.

Dorsal: Pertaining to the back; upper surface.

Dorsolateral: Pertaining to the upper sides.

Dorsum: The upper surface.

Ecological niche: The precise habitat utilized by a species.

Ectothermic: "Cold-blooded."

Endothermic: "Warm-blooded."

The bumblebee morph is one of several "bee" pattern types of the ball python.

A normal and an axanthic ball python coil together.

Form: An identifiable species or sub-species.

Genus: A taxonomic classification of a group of species having similar characteristics. The genus falls between the next higher designation of "family" and the next lower designation of "species." *Genera* is the plural of *genus*. It is always capitalized when written.

Glottis: The opening of the windpipe.

Granular: Pertaining to small, flat scales.

Gravid: The reptilian equivalent of mammalian pregnancy.

Gular: Pertaining to the throat.

Heliothermic: Pertaining to a species that basks in the sun to thermoregulate.

Hemipenes: The dual copulatory organs of male lizards and snakes.

Hemipenis: The singular form of *hemipenes*.

Herpetoculture: The captive breeding of reptiles and amphibians.

Herpetoculturist: One who indulges in herpetoculture.

Herpetologist: One who studies herpetology.

Herpetology: The study (often scientifically oriented) of reptiles and amphibians.

Hibernacula: Winter dens.

Hydrate: To restore body moisture by drinking or absorption.

Jacobson's organs: Highly enervated olfactory pits in the palate of snakes and lizards.

Juvenile: A young or immature specimen.

Labial: Pertaining to the lips.

Lateral: Pertaining to the side.

Melanism: A profusion of black pigment.

Mental: The scale at the tip of the lower lip.

Middorsal: Pertaining to the middle of the back.

Midventral: Pertaining to the center of the belly or abdomen.

Monotypic: Containing but one type.

Nocturnal: Active at night.

Oviparous: Reproducing by means of eggs that hatch after laying.

Parietal eye: A sensory organ positioned midcranially in certain reptiles.

Pelvic girdle: As used with boids, the vestigial bony girdle to which the remnants of hind limbs are attached.

Photoperiod: The daily/seasonally variable length of the hours of daylight.

Piebald: Having patches of stark white alternating randomly with normal pigmentation.

Poikilothermic: A species with no internal body temperature regulation. The old term was *cold-blooded*; ectothermic.

Postocular: To the rear of the eye.

Premaxillary: Bones at the front of the upper jaw.

Prey imprinting: Preferring prey of only a particular species and/or color.

Rostral: The (often modified) scale on the tip of the snout.

Scute: Scale.

Species: A group of similar creatures that produce viable young when breeding. The taxonomic designation that falls beneath "genus" and above "subspecies." Abbreviation, "sp."

Spur: As used with boids, the vestigial single "clawlike" appendage on each side of the anus. This is usually more prominent on male specimens than on females.

Taxonomy: The science of classification of plants and animals.

Terrestrial: Land-dwelling.

Thermoreceptive: Sensitive to heat.

Thermoregulate: To regulate (body) temperature by choosing a warmer or cooler environment.

Thigmothermic: Pertaining to a species (often nocturnal) that thermoregulates by being in contact with a preheated surface such as a boulder or tarred road surface.

Vent: The external opening of the cloaca; the anus.

Venter: The underside of a creature; the belly.

Ventral: Pertaining to the undersurface or belly.

Ventrolateral: Pertaining to the sides of the venter (belly).

Vestigial: Degenerated.

Other scientific definitions are contained in the following two volumes:

Peters, James A. 1964. *Dictionary of Herpetology*. New York: Hafner Publishing Co.

Wareham, David C. 1993. *The Reptile and Amphibian Keeper's Dictionary*. London: Blandford.

A normal ball python slowly crawls over a sandy patch of ground.

Index